COLORFUL SCARS

**The Woman Who Was Not
Poem By Shiloh Sophia
©2018**

www.colorful-scars.com

Table of Contents

Dedication

*This book dedicated to all women
who have had experiences
that have made you feel less than
you are. You are so much more than enough.*

A new day is here. Stepping into this new day often requires us to take inventory of our experiences. Followed by the healing that comes when we share our story. Once we have spoken and been witnessed by compassionate hearts, our healing journey accelerates and calls us forward.

For some of us, the next steps are found in circles of women, poetry, painting, dancing, drumming and howling at the moon.... It can be messy, sometimes rageful and will take the time it needs. And sometimes we don't let ourselves admit when we are complete.

I am here to ask you, to ask yourself:
Am I healed enough?
Sometimes we wait to believe in ourselves fully or to experience wholeness. We don't need to wait for the complete healing. Rather, healed

enough is enough. Of course, you are enough as you are now. Feeling complete with healing can be an illusive destination. As you well know, the journey is where healing happens - but we can get stuck in wanting to be done or feeling a certain way.

As for this poem, it felt to me as if I spoke from a collective of voices. Some of it is drawn from personal awareness, yet it is infused from what I have witnessed in working with women. Poetry can have its own life. Once you put pen to paper or keyboard, off it goes. I just let it come through. I felt it, I cried. I wanted to yell out these words, as that is how they felt in my soul. So this is not my story alone, but rather, a collective story. And perhaps part of a collective healing. I can hope.

The opening words for this poem woke me up one morning in the early darkness during a recent trip to Italy: "I am not a couch." I wondered what on earth I would do with that phrase. Then I remembered a line from one of my mother's poems in which she says:

"And then she became the furniture"
~ Caron McCloud

4

Part One: I Am Not

I am not a couch to be lounged upon

Not a bed with wrinkled sheets

I am not a chair in which to eat potato chips

Not a door to pass through casually

I am not a vessel waiting to be filled up

Not a cup, half full or half empty

With a chipped lip

I am not a place

To put things temporarily

Not a road to walk upon

Without reading the signs

I am not a doormat

For dirty boots

I am not a mere mark on a page

Not a window to look through

Not a means to an end

I am not graffiti, profane or otherwise

I am certainly not a toll free number

Seen from a beckoning freeway billboard

Not a bathroom wall with lipstick kisses

I am no bar serving drunken customers

With an empty red stool waiting for ass

I am simply not available for:

Placing, putting, storing, projecting,

Stuffing, shitting or sitting upon

Nor am I interested in

Labelling, marking, archetyping

Not a marketing image of

A diva going down

Did I mention

I am not a target audience?

Not a niche market or demographic

I am just not what you think

Let's start here

If we are to get anywhere

I am not a whim

Not a random muse to fixate upon

Designed for entertainment

Not a toy for playing with

I will not be conformed,

Distorted, contorted or consorted

I am no consort

Of misplaced desire or

Unwanted advances

I am no longer sorry to disappoint

No longer willing to be considered second

I do not hobble my hips with apology

Nor curdle my lips to kiss ass

Nor will I waste time,

Fighting systems that fight

What I love and serve

I step out of preconception, deception,

Conditional feminine frames

Internalized oppression, be gone!

Listen:

I take up too much space

For apologies now

Scars expand my presence

Such that I cannot be

Contained, strained, detained

Reframed, defamed or stained

Apologies were welcome before

But please, not right now!

I just want to occupy my space

Without giving face to the drama

I have derailed the runaway stories

That power such myths

This Venus on a half shell

Was not born from the foam of male gods

Out-dated myths of birth giving male gods

Have occupied our imaginations

For quite long enough

Thank you not so very much

There shall be no more deals

With underworlds or overlords

I eat pomegranates in dripping dozens

With no bargain sealed

I reunite with my mother

In every season, as I please,

We laugh at lesser negotiations

Rebel doesn't even begin to speak to

What I am now

Who am I now?

I have outgrown my default settings

With a clattering clash and crash, finally,

The façade has fallen

I am proudly a danger to

Society and small minds

Step back!

I am not a designer label

Not a car to drive fast

Not a hotel stay

Room service cannot be ordered here

My new robes are too large for

Double page spread magazine layouts

I don't fit the pictures anymore

My exile is complete

The Woman Who Was Not,

Who Now Is

Part Two: You Are Not

To those lovers that love me I say:

You are not the topic of this

Though I do include you

Even if you would rather not

There will be times for mutual apology

Time for sorting metaphors and memories

His and hers, theirs and ours, and us

Not today,

Yet I do have something to say

There is no need

To fall at my feet

Offer promises, talk of forever

I do not need white veils to look through

I do not need to be saved

I do not desire lip service

I am ready for the truth

Only the truth will do

Will you dare?

Do you think this is all about you?

This isn't about excluding you

I naturally do include you

A fine distinction

I don't have to make an exception

To include you

Do you?

Do you wonder what

This has cost you?

The cost between us

The loss lost between us

How it has hurt you

To allow me to hurt?

To not stand for truth, actively

Not passively

Not only when I am in the room

Stand for me when I am not looking

Because you want to

Because you know it is right

Not because it is correct do so

Or because now

You have no other choice

What I speak of is beyond careful tones

Of equality, of assigned gender roles

Of what each body is designed to do

When and with whom

Chances are, you have missed

What was hidden in plain sight,

Chances are, I did too

Did you?

I am not what you thought

You are not what I thought

I wanted you with all your danger

Can you want me with all of mine?

It takes time

I am willing

To sort through

Your shadows with you

Will you help me sort mine?

Things have gone missing

Now that I'm no longer a Ms. Anyone

I am a free woman

Whose secret name curls on her tongue

Sweetness enters the soul

When a woman finds her secret name

Women,

Don't rush to tell it

Don't ever sell it

Savour Your Self

There will be times for mutual apology

The sorting of metaphors and memories

His and hers, theirs and ours, and us

Not today

Today belongs to me

This is not about you

Today is re-membering

Into wholeness, no apologies

Do not try to rush me to nicety,

Hurry me to your ideas of justice

Do not clean up my language,

Correct my incorrectness,

Preserve my intelligence,

Or make an effort to save my reputation

I am beyond reputation

Finally freed!

My name, my body, my sex

Already assigned and maligned

With my decency

Finally released from keeping up

I become unacceptable

Questionable, a woman of ill repute

Suits me just fine

I am mine

I have the time

This time, this one time,

Do not tell me that men suffer too

You think I don't know?

I know, I feel all of this

Do not tell me

Women create violence too

You think I don't know who we are?

Who we have become?

We can be as wretched as we choose

I do know, I feel all of this

There are always exceptions

To accepted norms and patterns

I am speaking largely here

Of most and many women's experience

I am speaking to a culture where

Violation is sold as sexy

When unzipped jeans on young girls

Is allowable on billboards in the town square

From such a young age

This begins, and with it, hidden rage

We grow up hiding or flaunting or both

This has nothing,

Do you hear me?

Nothing to do with choosing to be sexy

Because a woman chooses to be

In her own sovereignty

When I speak of

Not being a couch, a chair or a bed,

Not being a road or a cup,

Neither a door or a window,

Not a mere vessel to be filled

I mean to speak of women

Specifically, uniquely, divinely

Feminine

My stand for myself

For all women

Does not negate

My stand for justice for all

My stand is not against,

My stand is for

For humanity, whole

Yet today, when I speak of

Not being a couch do not correct me

The woman who was not,

Who now is, will have cycles

Of anger, rage, dismay

She may misplace revenge

In the messy work of recovery

Seeking to be

The Woman Who Now Is

Stories told, hands to hold

Lives to unfold

This is a cycle of recovery

A turning towards beauty

Shrouded in story

Finding our glory takes time

When we are ready for visitors

It will be obvious because

You will be invited

Sculpt your ideas into roses

The scent of vast oceans and

Love larger than any sky

You have ever seen

Form new language

Invite new eyes to see

Step out of old patterns

Be willing to change frames

Be willing to have no idea

How this goes

This is not about earning a place

This is about honouring our space

There is learning to do

Yes I am willing to teach you

Are you willing to learn?

Your previous club membership

Has been revoked,

But may be able to be renewed

Some may have thought

We were high maintenance before

Mistaking our needs for frills or cheap thrills

Laughing at our requests for sustenance

The need for beauty, order, quiet

The hungering for attention attended to

The showing up of your soul

We tried to tell you

Speaking into entrenched trenches

Part Three: We Are Not

To those who have hurt us

Without really knowing how this works

We implore you, to explore you

Woman

Most precious image

Uplifted as sex symbol, idol, ideal

Simultaneously shaped as a product

Consummated, consumed

Disposed of, repurposed as

Hips, lips, and curves,

Used, abused, posed and poised,

Praised and shamed, defamed,

Flayed and played

The paradox is a mystery made of

Madness and mixed messages

We are cherished and crushed

Scattered, clearly no serious matter

Divided and conquered, no more!

You must have mistaken us

For someplace or someone else

You may have thought us familiar at first

Yet we are not what you know

Or ever have known

We are the women

Who were not,

Who now are

Who we have become is

Not on any map

Beyond our edges

There be dragons

That breathes holy fire shaped by

Every intrusion, suggestion,

Projection, titillation, perpetration,

Forged by unwanted words

The shapes we are now

Are new shapes

Step back!

We need room to move!

Our colorful scars emit blinding light

Only kindness, in supple shimmer,

Awareness spoken by beings of insight

Is permitted near these temples

Likely that will exclude you

Perhaps a few

Did we mention,

We are not to be trenched,

Wenched, or benched,

Trifles to be fetched?

The ditch has already been dug

Put down your shovel

When we speak of you

We do not speak of every single one

We speak with broad strokes

Of culture, tradition, sanction,

Status quo, those in the know,

Know who they are

We are done with trying to get it right

This is not a punishment

This is not a typical accusation

Not a he said, she said

This is not meant to inspire fear

Nor to divide and conquer

We just wanted you to know:

We are not the furniture

A new relationship with women

Who were not...who now are

Is born today!

We Do Declare It!

Part Four: Here We Are

A birth of thousands, millions,

Galaxies of women, gushing forth

From the collective womb of awareness

The largest birth canal the Earth has known,

Stunning even the stars!

The constellations blink in awe

The milky way offers her infinite breasts

To nurture us, grow us mighty and strong

We are awareness made matter,

Beauty walking and waking and finding form

Found in every color, we are, brilliant!

Astonishing, glorious, joyously infamous!

If you can't see us yet, try sunglasses

This brightness only blinds when

You haven't been taught how to see

How to see with what kind of seeing

How to be, with what kinds of being

What you call complicated,

We see as holy,

Facets of the whole

Our sovereignty and dignity can create unity

In recent unfortunate world events

Our fortune has been forged

In the stories of women of me too

No longer told in hushed tones

With authorities that provide

Useful context for suffering

When we expose ourselves,

Shamelessly, that is, without shame,

Stories baring teeth

Songs stamped out with bare feet

We herald a new day, a new way

Let the news spread

We are coming forth!

Part Five: Not Your Soul

We can change this

Mend this, heal our past

Your soul is not the problem

You are not damaged goods

This story does not live in soul

Hear this:

Hidden bias is called that

Because it is hidden

What we need now is

Intelligence about our conditioning

Willingness to see privilege

Built into culture, that goes

Unchecked and assumed

What we need now,

To survive and thrive

Is freedom from 'power over' systems

We will not thrive in systems

That requires one to overpower another

This is not an easy template to shake

Is the payoff worth the risk?

Can we be ourselves otherwise?

For us,

Flattered, afraid, assaulted by

Too toxic cocktails of admiration

Where witnessing beauty

Becomes an aggression

Spoken or silent:

"If I can't have you

Then you must go down"

This has gone on too long

We have always known, even when

Our knowing was frozen in fear:

Lip service without soul

Fails us all

In many cultures ancient and new

In towns of rednecks or red neckties

Women feel they have no choice

Women face death, rape, abuses

Beyond measure

Now is our time of recovery

Recognition is finally here

We are seen and we also see

Those who can, must rise!

As we rise

We call the others up!

Awakening is what opens us now

I know what I am and am not

This is not my soul or yours

This does not live in souls

This lives in belief

We can change minds

In this there is hope

In this we engage in soul work

The willing soul

Will change

You do not need to be offended

You do not need to defend or pretend

Let us mend

Let us mend

Let us mend

Part Six: This is Not

This is not an apology

Not a request, not an invitation

This is not a suggestion or divination

Let this be my declaration

Let each woman sing out, differently,

Yet in this agreeing: We are free

If the lovers and the fighters

Could see this:

That in our freedom they are freed,

There would be no need for me,

To say:

I Am the Woman

Who Was Not, Who Now Is

I have offered here

Much of what I am not

Speaking out from the silence

So that I could find what I am

In the saying so, and in the being so,

I have found me

This is intentional creativity

Through the process of diving in

We begin and begin to see

This is not about you

This time it is about me

Here is what I need:

Willingness to stand

Willingness to see

Willingness to be free

In my freedom,

You are free

This is the way of women

This desire for willingness

Has been here always

In my way I have spoken it

Maybe my voice was lost in noise

Maybe I didn't know how to shape it

Or you didn't know how to hear it, then

We are both subject to fallacy,

To prophecy, false morality,

Ideals of Adam's destiny

Believe this: A new day for me

Can be a new day for you

My voice will speak for more than just me

For justice is in me

I am not a couch to be lounged upon

Not a bed with wrinkled sheets

I am not a chair in which to eat potato chips

Not a door to pass through casually

I am not a vessel waiting to be filled up

Not a cup, half full or half empty

With a chipped lip

I Am the Woman

Who Was Not

Who Is Now

Part Seven: Not Your Problem

To those who would say

This is not your problem

Not your jam

Not your experience

Not your political leaning

Let us be very clear:

This is everyone's problem

Until this is solved

We all suffer

If you do not see this

You are not looking

Chances are that thinking this is:

Not your problem

Has cost you the gift of intimacy

And true love with your lovers

We treat the earth

Like we treat women

The place we came from

The place we live

We allow to be polluted

When will you take part?

When?

Part Eight: Now What

Sisters, we have long worn our scars

On the inside, hidden within ourselves

Doing our best to hide,

To not allow them

To show up on the outside

We didn't want to be exposed,

Judged, blamed and not believed

Our souls bear the marks

Of re-membering what was lost

We have been shaped, girdled, silenced,

Fragmented and shamed into looking good

That we learned from our wounds

Is not the question, that we called

Harm on ourselves is the issue

Dear precious soul,

If you have carried the thought that you,

have caused your own harm...

This is an invitation to lay it down for good

To release your grip on self blame

Self blame cloaked as responsibility

Has done more damage

Than we can imagine

Do you see how believing that you

Called it upon yourself,

Can keep you from speaking?

The dominant culture keeps this idea in place

We know better, and can release ourselves

We have already turned our wounds

Into teachings for ourselves and others

Are you ready to let go of this part

Of the wounding you carry?

Is it time?

When scars are only on the inside

They can take a long time to heal

We can choose rather to integrate,

Indeed they have informed us

The colorful side of all of these stories

Is that the scars

Are no longer only on the inside

Witness by compassionate hearts brings color

To the shadows which house the wounds

The light emitting from our colorful scars

Illuminates the path for those coming after us

A warrior mark, a reminder, a tattoo

Of teachings and stories to tell

We won't forget, yet neither will we

Be jailed by the past any longer

To those who would harm,

We also pray, this colorful light

Invites them to think again and to heal

The freedom to self-express

This is a basic human right

We claim this right for ourselves

We won't proclaim the bright side

We will not dwell in the shadow side either

We see, claim and are

Authors of the colorful side

We have become

She of the Colorful Scar

With hope for

re-membering our wholeness

Part Nine: I Am

I have arrived

In all my glory flowing

All my color glowing

All my stories shining

I am here

I am who I am

I will be discovering her

She who has not lived out loud

Will speak her truth

I have arrived

I Am the Woman

Who Was Not

Who Is Now

Letter To My Sisters

Just like moons and like suns,
With the certainty of tides,
Just like hopes springing high,
Still I'll rise ~ Maya Angelou

October 2018
Porto Venere, Italy - The Port of Venus

Sparked by Ford - Kavanaugh experience and how it impacted my community. This is the letter I sent with the first draft of the poem.

Dear Sister,

I send new moon greetings from Italy where I am here working with women on the Divine Feminine – our stories, ideas, wounds, teachings, and how we can each do our own work of healing and transformation. So many layers.

I have been thinking of you, and of all of us – and especially right now my sisters in the United States who have been so impacted by the recent happenings. I don't think I need to spell it out – regardless of what you think about it – it was traumatizing for most of us it seems.

I could feel it and see it in ways I haven't for a while. Like wow – where do we live? I looked at the images of the people involved ands sent them love – all of them. All of them. I felt called to DO SOMETHING to serve – hence Colorful Scars – a poem and class for us as a community. I asked: What I could do? I had already painted the painting – and so it was clear – Colorful Scars it would be. Claiming our wounds and bringing beauty to them. Covering them in grace – not hiding – but lifting them up.

I try to be mindful of sharing spiritual beliefs without assumptive behaviours, which are so often rampant. Even just – 'everything happens for a reason' is a rampant spiritual belief gone unchecked that a lot of us don't agree with. Including me. So I am writing to you with permission to set yourself free from the way you have been carrying what has happened to you.

I share this writing and class for those who still think they are to blame for their abuse. This is FOR YOU. For us to heal.

With respect to those in the sisterhood that truly believe they agreed to their own harm at the level of soul, I hear you. And. What is true for you might be true for you. Yet I might add, do not assume it is also true for everyone else. This teaching is too common, and in my view, assumptive and often unconscious.

Now, having worked with so many women I am a stand for freedom from self-blame – and the idea that we caused our own harm as part of our path or soul agreement. Not that there aren't times we have put ourselves in danger and harm's way. Each story has its own arc of blame and shame.

I stand for a story where no woman blames herself for being harmed in ANY scenario.

I woke up this morning with the collective grief pouring through me. I thought, is there a bright side? And of course, the bright side is that the stories are being told and that hopefully those who do the harming will think again instead of become even more aggressive, which is often the case. Yet, bright side, felt too optimistic. Shadow side is obviously playing itself out before our eyes in the United States and many other places. But the colorful side, is also here. Finding our freedom from suppression and silence – finding self-expression. Why is this important? Because if we are self-expressed, we won't bottle up the energy and turn it on ourselves. Expressing it lets it out – and in that, changes it as it moves from within to the page/ canvas /dance floor/ pottery wheel.

I am thinking of you and however you process what you are feeling. Let us walk this road together in the best way we can.

I want to thank my husband Jonathan, who gave me so many ideas to work with in this writing. His willingness to look with me, is truly astonishing, and I have learned so much from him about the hidden dynamics. As a chef and a soldier he has seen what he calls 'the worst of what there is'

I also want to give thanks to my Intentional Creativity community, The Red Thread Cafe classroom for being such powerful parts of the story and the healing. Thank you to my editor, Ti Klingler who rocked the first edition of this poem with fierce kindness. With editing support from Fiona Catsea Wilde and Michaelanne Gephart. And Sarah Mardell for helping me share the class that goes with this poem. I feel so blessed to be surrounded by women who are doing their work.

SIGNED WITH A RED THREAD, SHILOH SOPHIA

About Shiloh Sophia

Shiloh Sophia lives life as a great adventure! A renaissance woman who communicates her philosophy through paintings, poetry, teachings and entrepreneurship. For 25 years she has dedicated her soul work to the study and practice of creativity as a path of healing which provides access to consciousness.

As a curator and gallery owner, she has represented her own work, as well as hundreds of women artists. By the age of 40 she achieved incredible success through being in the top ten percent of sales for contemporary artists in the U.S. Her prolific intuitive painting process led to a desire to teach and provided the foundation for the ground-breaking work on how Intentional Creativity® can give voice to the soul. Her method of 'creating with mindfulness' has reached tens of thousands of students who have gained insight into the hidden self.

Her work is taught widely, at university in MA and PhD programs, the United Nations CSW, and by hundreds of Certified Teachers. At the core of her work is a belief that the right to self express is one of the most basic human rights – "We have a right to know how to access what we think, feel, believe and to express it in our lives" Her life path is a spiritual practice, and an offering that was awakened through feminine Divine. Her research dives into the exploration of the right/left brain connection with the heart and re-inventing personal archetypes as gateways to liberation. "When we find freedom from the trauma of our stories, we can invent our own legends, and do the sacred work of organizing our consciousness."

She is the creator of seven illustrated books, as well as a community leader. Having been trained by her mother Caron McCloud, the poet, and Sue Hoya Sellars, the artist, she brought her gifts of language and image into form through founding the Intentional Creativity ® Guild, Cosmic Cowgirls®, and Color of Woman®. She lives and works in Carmel, California.

Her school, which she founded with her husband Jonathan provides education both in house and online, reaching over 25k subscribers a month. She can be found most days having tea with her muses and Siamese kitties discussing quantum physics and celebrating revelations of the heart.

She lives and teaches a philosophy that all art forms are tools for individual, social and spiritual transformation. She has taught her curriculum at universities including California Institute for Integral Studies and the Institute for Transpersonal Psychology in the MA and Global PhD programs. She has conducted research with hundreds of people and on the impact creativity can have on their lives for healing and insight.

Shiloh's paintings are internationally collected and her product line is represented at galleries and fine shops throughout the United States. She has spoken at the United Nations at the Commission on the Status of Women in 2013,14,15,16,17 and has articles published in the global outlets that serve women like Women News Network and WUNRN. She also illustrates books, including Alice Walker's book on poetry, Hard Times Require Furious Dancing.

She and her husband Jonathan travel the world together providing experiences for others in food, art, and conversation.

Every bone in your body is a creative bone.

To order copies of the book or take the free class: www.colorful-scars.com

www.shilohsophia.com to learn more about the author.

95343632R00035

Made in the USA
Middletown, DE
26 October 2018